A Play in

Twelve An

by

REGINALD ROSE

Stage Version by SHERMAN L. SERGEL

Adapted from the Television Show
"Twelve Angry Men"
Initially presented on
STUDIO ONE, CBS-TV

THE DRAMATIC PUBLISHING COMPANY

TWELVE ANGRY WOMEN

A Play in Three Acts

FOR FIFTEEN WOMEN

CHARACTERS

FOREMAN OF THE JURY
JUROR NO. TWO
JUROR NO. THREE
JUROR NO. FOUR
JUROR NO. FIVE
JUROR NO. SIX
JUROR NO. SEVEN
JUROR NO. EIGHT
JUROR NO. NINE
JUROR NO. TEN
JUROR NO. ELEVEN
JUROR NO. TWELVE
GUARD (*bit part*)
JUDGE (*bit part*) } *offstage voices*
CLERK (*bit part*) }

PLACE: *A jury room.*

TIME: *The present. Summer.*

SYNOPSIS

ACT ONE: *Late afternoon.*

ACT TWO: *A second or two later.*

ACT THREE: *Immediately following Act Two.*

NOTES ON CHARACTERS
AND COSTUMES

FOREMAN: She is a small, petty woman who is impressed with the authority she has and handles herself quite formally. She is not overly bright, but dogged.

JUROR NO. TWO: She is a meek, hesitant woman who finds it difficult to maintain any opinion of her own. She is easily swayed and usually adopts the opinion of the last person to whom she has spoken.

JUROR NO. THREE: She is a very strong, very forceful, extremely opinionated woman, within whom can be detected a streak of sadism. Also, she is a humorless woman who is intolerant of opinions other than her own, and accustomed to forcing her wishes and views upon others.

JUROR NO. FOUR: She seems to be a woman of wealth and position, and a practiced speaker who presents herself well at all times. She seems to feel a little bit above the rest of the jurors. Her only concern is with the facts in this case, and she is appalled with the behavior of the others.

JUROR NO. FIVE: She is a naive, very frightened young woman who takes her obligations in this case very seriously but who finds it difficult to speak up when her elders have the floor.

JUROR NO. SIX: She is an honest but dull-witted woman who comes upon her decisions slowly and carefully. She is a woman who finds it difficult to create positive opinions, but who must listen to and digest and accept those opinions offered by others which appeal to her most.

JUROR NO. SEVEN: She is a loud, flashy, glad-handing woman who works in a department store and has more important things to do than to sit on a jury. She is quick to show temper, quick to form opinions on things about which she knows nothing. She is a bully and, of course, a coward.

JUROR NO. EIGHT: She is a quiet, thoughtful, gentle woman

4

—a woman who sees all sides of every question and constantly seeks the truth. She is a woman of strength tempered with compassion. Above all, she is a woman who wants justice to be done, and will fight to see that it is.

JUROR NO. NINE: She is a mild, gentle old woman, long since defeated by life and now merely waiting to die. She recognizes herself for what she is, and mourns the days when it would have been possible to be courageous without shielding herself behind her many years.

JUROR NO. TEN: She is an angry, bitter woman—a woman who antagonizes almost at sight. She is also a bigot who places no value on any human life save her own. Here is a woman who has been nowhere and is going nowhere, and knows it deep within herself.

JUROR NO. ELEVEN: She is a refugee from Europe, who came to this country in 1941. She speaks with an accent and is ashamed, humble, almost subservient to the people around her. She will honestly seek justice, because she has suffered through so much injustice.

JUROR NO. TWELVE: She is a slick, bright advertising woman who thinks of human beings in terms of percentages, graphs and polls, and has no real understanding of people. She is a superficial snob, but is trying to be companionable.

GUARD: This is a bit part. She can be a policewoman, of any age.

CHART OF STAGE POSITIONS

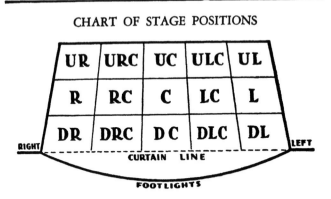

STAGE POSITIONS

Upstage means away from the footlights, *downstage* means toward the footlights, and *right* and *left* are used with reference to the actor as he faces the audience. R means *right*, L means *left*, U means *up*, D means *down*, C means *center*, and these abbreviations are used in combination, as: U R for *up right*, R C for *right center*, D L C for *down left center*, etc. One will note that a position designated on the stage refers to a general territory, rather than to a given point.

NOTE: Before starting rehearsals, chalk off your stage or rehearsal space as indicated above in the *Chart of Stage Positions*. Then teach your actors the meanings and positions of these fundamental terms of stage movement by having them walk from one position to another until they are familiar with them. The use of these abbreviated terms in directing the play saves time, speeds up rehearsals, and reduces the amount of explanation the director has to give to his actors.

STAGE CHART

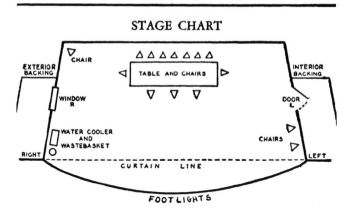

PROPERTIES

GENERAL: Long conference table and twelve straight chairs, electric clock, water cooler, container for paper cups, wastebasket, three other straight chairs, pads of paper, pencils and ashtrays on table. NOTE: Some of the jurors have cigarettes and matches. All carry handbags.

FIVE: Knitting.

GUARD: Key for door, switch knife with tag, diagram of apartment.

SEVEN: Gum, handkerchief.

THREE: Crocheting, pencil, skirt pattern.

FOREMAN: Paper for balloting, pencil and paper.

TEN: Handkerchief.

TWELVE: Compact, pencil.

EIGHT: Notes, switch knife.

TWO: Box of cough drops, glasses.

FOUR: Handkerchief, glasses.

PRODUCTION NOTE

Nothing adds more to the polish of a production than the quick picking up of cues. Unless there is a definite reason for a pause, train your actors to come in with their speeches "on the heels," so to speak, of the preceding speeches. When a production lags, audience interest likewise will lag.

It is always advisable during the last week of rehearsals to hold one or more sessions during which the actors merely sit around in a circle and go through lines only with the express purpose of snapping up cues.

NOTE

Twelve Angry Women may also be performed as *Twelve Angry Men*. Or by using a combination of these two editions, it can be staged with a mixed cast as *Twelve Angry Jurors*.

Should you wish to produce the play using a cast of eight women and five men, you would order eight copies of **Code T43** (*Twelve Angry Women*) and five copies of **Code T42** (*Twelve Angry Men*). Distribute the parts to suit the individual talents of the particular performers. You may use any combination of men and women totaling thirteen.

Because the pagination of the two editions differs, some directors prefer to order all one version and only one copy of the other version, notating changes in the individual scripts where necessary. The choice is yours. We do encourage you to order a preview copy of each edition in order to determine what will best serve your particular requirements.

The key parts to watch in casting are the parts of **Jurors #3 and #8**. These should probably be played by men, if you have them available—though any combination of men and women you have available will work.

ACT ONE

AT RISE OF CURTAIN: *The curtain comes up on a dark stage; then as the lights start to come up on the scene we hear the voice of the* JUDGE, *offstage.*]

JUDGE [*offstage*]. Murder in the first degree . . . premeditated homicide . . . is the most serious charge tried in our criminal courts. You have heard a long and complex case, ladies, and it is now your duty to sit down to try to separate the facts from the fancy. One man is dead. The life of another is at stake. If there is a reasonable doubt in your minds as to the guilt of the accused—then you must declare him not guilty. If—however—there is no reasonable doubt, then he must be found guilty. Whichever way you decide, the verdict must be unanimous. I urge you to deliberate honestly and thoughtfully. You are faced with a grave responsibility. Thank you, ladies.

[*There is a long pause. The lights are now up full in the jury room. There is a door* L *and a window in the* R *wall of the room. Over the door* L *is an electric clock. A water cooler is* D R, *with a wastebasket beside it. A container with paper cups is attached to the wall nearby. A long conference table is slightly upstage of* C *stage. About it are twelve uncomfortable-looking straight chairs. There are a chair at either end of the table, seven at the upstage side and three at the downstage side of the table.* (NOTE: *This arrangement of the chairs about the table will enable most of the action to be directed toward the audience, with a minority of the characters placed with their backs toward the audience.*) *There are two more straight chairs against the wall* D L *and one in the* U R *corner of the room. It is a bare, unpleasant room. After the pause the door* L *opens and the* GUARD

9

*walks in. As she opens the door the lettering "Jury Room"
can be seen on the outside of the door. The* GUARD *walks
across the room and opens the window* R *as a clerk drones
out, offstage* L.]

CLERK [*offstage* L]. The jury will retire.
GUARD [*surveying room, shaking her head*]. He doesn't stand
a chance. [*Moves* L *again.*]

[*The* JURORS *file in* L. *The* GUARD *stands upstage of the door
and counts them. Four or five of the jurors light cigarettes
as they enter the room.* JUROR FIVE *takes out some knitting,
on which she works constantly.* JURORS TWO, NINE, *and*
TWELVE *go to the water cooler for a drink.* JUROR SEVEN
goes to the window and opens it wider. The rest of the
JURORS *begin to take seats around the table, though two of
them stand behind their chairs, and others lean forward,
with both hands on the back of the chair.* JUROR SEVEN
*produces a pack of gum and offers a piece to the women by
the water cooler.*]

SEVEN. Chewing gum? Gum? Gum?
NINE. Thank you, but no. [JURORS TWO *and* TWELVE *shake
their heads.*]
SEVEN. Y'know something?
TWELVE. I know lots of things. I'm in advertising.
SEVEN. Y'know, it's hot. [*Takes out handkerchief, dabs at
perspiration on face.*]
TWELVE [*to* TWO, *mildly sarcastic*]. I never would have known
that if she hadn't told me. Would you?
TWO [*missing sarcasm*]. I suppose not. I'd kind of forgotten.
TWELVE. All I've done all day is perspire.
THREE [*calling out*]. I bet you aren't perspiring like that boy
who was tried.
SEVEN. You'd think they'd at least air-condition the place. I
almost died in court.
TWELVE. My taxes are high enough.
SEVEN. This should go fast, anyway. [*Moves to table, as* EIGHT
goes to window.]

NINE [*nodding to herself, then, as she throws her paper water cup into the wastebasket*]. Yes, it's hot.

GUARD. All right, ladies. Everybody's here. If there's anything you want, I'm right outside. Just knock. [*Goes out L, closing door. They all look at door, silently. The lock is turned.*]

THREE. Did she lock that door?

FOUR. Yes, she did.

THREE. What do they think we are, crooks?

FOREMAN [*seated at left end of table*]. They lock us up for a little while. . . .

THREE [*interrupting*]. And then they lock that boy up forever, and that's all right with me. [*Takes out crocheting and begins to work on it.*]

FIVE [*motioning toward door*]. I never knew they did that.

TEN [*blowing her nose*]. Sure, they lock the door. What did you think?

FIVE [*a bit irritated*]. I just didn't know. It never occurred to me.

FOUR. Shall we all admit right now that it is hot and humid and our tempers are short?

EIGHT [*turning from window*]. It's been a pretty hard week. [*Turns back and continues to look out.*]

THREE. I feel just fine, so long as I've got my crocheting.

TWELVE. I wonder what's been going on down at the office. You know how it is in advertising. In six days my job could be gone—and the whole company, too. They aren't going to like this. [*JURORS start to take off their suit coats, jackets, gloves, etc. Two of them start to fan themselves.*]

FOREMAN. Well, I think this is our duty.

TWELVE. I didn't object to doing my duty. I just mentioned that I might not have a job by the time I get back. [*She and NINE move to table and take their places. NINE sits near right end of table.*]

THREE [*motioning to FOUR*]. Ask her to help you. She's rich. I bet her husband could give you a wonderful job. Look at that outfit!

FOREMAN [*to* FOUR, *as she tears off slips of paper for a ballot*]. Is it an original?

FOUR. Yes, it is.

FOREMAN. I have an aunt who makes dresses. [FOUR *takes off her hat and gloves.*]

FOUR. How does she do?

FOREMAN [*shaking her head*]. Not too well. You know, a friend of hers, that's a friend of my aunt, the dressmaker, well, this friend wanted to be on this jury in my place.

SEVEN. Why didn't you let her? I'd have done anything to miss this.

FOREMAN. And get caught, or something? You know what kind of a fine you could pay for a thing like that? Anyway, this friend of my aunt's was on a jury once, about ten years ago, a case just about like this one.

TWELVE. So, what happened?

FOREMAN. They let him off. Reasonable doubt. And do you know, about eight years later they found out that he'd actually done it, anyway. A guilty man, a murderer, was turned loose in the streets.

SEVEN. How horrible.

THREE. Did they get him?

FOUR. They couldn't.

THREE. Why not?

FOUR. No one can be held in double jeopardy. Unless it's a hung jury, they can't try anyone twice for the same crime.

SEVEN. That isn't going to happen here.

THREE. Six days. They should have finished it in two. [*Emphasizes with her crocheted material.*] Talk! Talk! Talk! [*Gets up and starts for the water cooler.*] Did you ever hear so much talk about nothing?

TWO [*laughing nervously*]. Well—I guess—they're entitled. . . .

THREE. Everybody gets a fair trial. . . . [*Shakes her head.*] That's the system. [*Drinks.*] Well, I suppose you can't say anything against it. [*Tosses her water cup toward the waste-*

basket and misses. TWO *picks up cup and puts it in basket, as* THREE *returns to her seat.*]

SEVEN [*to* TEN]. How did you like that business about the knife? Did you ever in your life hear such a story!

TEN [*wisely*]. Well, look, you have to expect that. You know what you're dealing with. . . .

SEVEN. He bought a switch knife that night.

TEN [*with a sneer*]. And then claimed he lost it!

SEVEN [*derisively*]. A hole in his pocket!

TEN. A hole in his father.

SEVEN. Men!

TWO. An awful way to kill your father—a knife in his chest. [*Crosses to table.*]

TEN. Look at the kind of people they are—you know them. [*Takes out handkerchief.*]

SEVEN. What's the matter? You got a cold?

TEN [*blowing*]. A lulu! These hot weather colds can kill you.

SEVEN. I had one last year. On my vacation, too!

FOREMAN [*briskly*]. All right, ladies. Let's take seats.

SEVEN. Right. This better be fast. I've got tickets to—[*Insert name of any current Broadway hit.*]—for tonight. My husband and I must be the only people in the whole world who haven't seen it yet. [*Laughs and sits down.*] Okay, your honor, start the show.

FOREMAN [*to* EIGHT, *who is still looking out the window*]. How about sitting down? [EIGHT *doesn't hear her.*] The lady at the window. [EIGHT *turns, startled.*] How about sitting down?

EIGHT. Oh, I'm sorry. [*Sits at right end of table, opposite* FOREMAN.]

TEN. It's hard to figure, isn't it? A boy kills his father. Bing! Just like that. Well, it's this juvenile delinquency. People let their children run wild. Maybe it serves 'em right.

FOUR. There's no point in getting emotional about it. It's a question of evidence—not how we feel.

SEVEN. We all agreed that it was hot.

NINE. And that our tempers will get short.

THREE. That's if we disagree—but this is open and shut. Let's get it done.

FOREMAN. All right. Now, you ladies can handle this any way you want to. I mean, I'm not going to make any rules. If we want to discuss it first and then vote, that's one way. Or we can vote right now to see how we stand.

SEVEN. Let's vote now. Who knows, maybe we can all go home.

TEN. Yeah. Let's see who's where.

THREE. Right. Let's vote now.

EIGHT. All right. Let us vote.

FOREMAN. Anybody doesn't want to vote? [*Looks around table. There is a pause as* ALL *look at each other.*]

SEVEN. That was easy.

FOREMAN. Okay. All those voting guilty raise your hands. [JURORS THREE, SEVEN, TEN *and* TWELVE *put their hands up instantly. The* FOREMAN *and* TWO, FOUR, FIVE *and* SIX *follow a second later. Then* ELEVEN *raises her hand, and a moment later* NINE *puts her hand up.*] Eight—nine—ten—eleven—that's eleven for guilty. Okay. Not guilty? [EIGHT'S *hand goes up.* ALL *turn to look at her.*]

THREE. Say, what's the matter with you?

FOREMAN. Okay. Eleven to one. Eleven guilty, one not guilty. Now we know where we stand.

THREE [*rising and standing up behind table, to* EIGHT]. Do you really believe he's not guilty?

EIGHT [*quietly*]. I don't know.

SEVEN [*to* FOREMAN]. After six days, she doesn't know.

TWELVE. In six days I could learn calculus. This is A,B,C.

EIGHT. I don't believe it's as simple as A,B,C.

THREE. I never saw a guiltier man in my life.

EIGHT. What does a guilty man look like? He is not guilty until we say he is guilty. Are we to vote on his face?

THREE. You sat right in court and heard the same things as I did. The boy's a dangerous killer. You could see it.

EIGHT. Where do you look, to see if someone is a killer?

THREE [*flouncing into her chair, irritated*]. Oh, well! [*Resumes her crocheting.*]

EIGHT [*with quiet insistence*]. I would like to know. Tell me what the facial characteristics of a killer are. Maybe you know something I don't know.

FOUR. Look, what is there about the case that makes you think the boy is innocent?

EIGHT. He's nineteen years old.

THREE. That's old enough. He knifed his own father. Four inches into the chest. An innocent little nineteen-year-old—murderer!

FOUR [*to* THREE]. I agree with you that the boy is guilty, but I think we should try to avoid emotionally colored arguments.

THREE. All right. They proved it a dozen different ways. Do you want me to list them?

EIGHT. No.

TEN [*rising, to* EIGHT]. Well, do you believe that stupid story he told?

FOUR [*to* TEN]. Now, now.

TEN. Do you believe the boy's story?

EIGHT. I don't know whether I believe it or not. Maybe I don't.

SEVEN. So what'd you vote not guilty for?

EIGHT. There were eleven votes for guilty—it's not so easy for me to raise my hand and send a boy off to die without talking about it first.

SEVEN. Who says it's easy for me?

FOUR. Or me?

EIGHT. No one.

FOREMAN. He's still just as guilty, whether it's an easy vote or a hard one.

SEVEN [*belligerently*]. Is there something wrong because I voted fast?

EIGHT. Not necessarily.

SEVEN. I think the boy's guilty. You couldn't change my mind if you talked for a hundred years.

EIGHT. I don't want to change your mind.

THREE. All right. What do you want?

EIGHT. I want to talk a while. Look, this boy's been kicked around all his life. You know, living in a slum, his mother dead since he was nine. He's a tough, angry boy. You know why slum children get that way? Because we knock them over the head all the time. I think maybe we owe him a few words. That's all. [*Looks around the table. She is met by cold looks.* JUROR NINE *nods slowly.* TWELVE *takes out her compact and puts on fresh make-up.*]

FOUR. All right, life's hard. It was hard for me. Everything we've got, my husband and I fought for. I worked my way through college, where I met him. That was a long time ago, and perhaps you do forget. I fought, yes. My husband fought. But neither of us ever killed.

THREE. I know what hard luck's like, but I never killed nobody, either.

TWELVE [*snaps compact shut*]. I've been kicked around, too. Wait until you've worked in an ad agency and the guy that buys the advertising walks in!

ELEVEN [*who speaks with an accent*]. In my country, in Europe, kicking was a science, but let's try to find something better than that.

TEN [*to* EIGHT]. I don't mind telling you this, sister. We don't owe the boy a thing. He got a fair trial, didn't he? You know what that trial cost? He's lucky he got it. Look, we're all grown-ups here. You're not going to tell us that we're supposed to believe him, knowing what he is. I've lived among 'em all my life. You can't believe a word they say. You know that.

NINE [*to* TEN, *very slowly*]. I don't know that. What a terrible thing to believe! Since when is dishonesty a group characteristic? You don't have a monopoly on the truth! . . .

THREE [*interrupting*]. All right. Save it for Sunday! We don't need a sermon.

NINE [*not heeding*]. What this woman says is very dangerous.

[EIGHT *puts her hand on* NINE'S *arm and stops her.* NINE *draws a deep breath and relaxes.*]

FOUR. I don't see any need for arguing like this. I think we ought to behave like ladies.

SEVEN. Right!

TWELVE [*smiling up at* FOUR]. Certainly, if you insist.

FOUR [*to* TWELVE]. Thank you.

TWELVE. Sure.

FOUR. If we're going to discuss this case, why, let's discuss the facts.

FOREMAN. I think that's a good point. We have a job to do. Let's do it.

ELEVEN. If you ladies don't mind, I'm going to close the window. [*Gets up and does so; then, apologetically, as she moves back to table.*] It was blowing on my neck. [TEN *blows her nose fiercely, as* ELEVEN *sits again.*]

SEVEN. *I'd* like to have the window open.

ELEVEN. But it was blowing on me.

SEVEN. Don't you want a little air? It's summer—it's hot.

ELEVEN. I was very uncomfortable.

SEVEN. There are twelve of us in this room; it's the only window. If you don't mind!

ELEVEN. I have some rights, too.

SEVEN. So do the rest of us.

FOUR [*to* ELEVEN]. Couldn't you trade chairs with someone at the other end of the table?

ELEVEN. All right, I will open the window, if someone would trade. [*Goes to window, opens it.* TWO *gets up and goes to* ELEVEN'S *chair, near right end of table.*]

TWO [*motioning*]. Take my chair.

ELEVEN. Thank you. [*Goes to* TWO'S *chair.*]

FOREMAN. Shall we get back to the case?

THREE. Yeah, let's.

TWELVE. I may have an idea here. I'm just thinking out loud now, but it seems to me that it's up to us to convince this lady—[*Indicates* EIGHT.]—that we're right and she's

wrong. Maybe if we each talk for a minute or two. You
know—try it on for size.

FOREMAN. That sounds fair enough.

FOUR. Very fair.

FOREMAN. Supposing we go once around the table.

SEVEN. Okay—let's start it off.

FOREMAN. Right. [*To* TWO.] I guess you're first.

TWO [*timidly*]. Oh, well. . . . [*There is a long pause.*] I
just think he's guilty. I thought it was obvious.

EIGHT. In what way was it obvious?

TWO. I mean that nobody proved otherwise.

EIGHT [*quietly*]. Nobody has to prove otherwise; innocent
until proven guilty. The burden of proof is on the prosecu-
tion. The defendant doesn't have to open his mouth. That's
in the Constitution. The Fifth Amendment. You've heard
of it.

FOUR. Everyone has.

TWO [*flustered*]. Well, sure—I've heard of it. I know what
it is . . . I . . . what I meant . . . well, anyway . . .
I think he's guilty.

EIGHT [*looking at* TWO, *shaking her head slowly*]. No reasons
—just guilty. There is a life at stake here.

THREE [*putting aside crocheting, picking up pencil and rapping smartly with it as she makes her points*]. Okay, let's
get to the facts. Number one, let's take that old man who
lives on the floor right underneath the room where the
murder took place. At ten minutes after twelve on the
night of the killing he heard loud noises in the upstairs
apartment. He said it sounded like a fight. Then he heard
the boy say to his father, "I'm gonna kill you." A second
later he heard a body falling, and he ran to the door of his
apartment, looked out, and saw the kid running downstairs
and out of the house. Then he called the police. They found
the father with a knife in his chest.

FOREMAN. And the coroner fixed the time of death at around
midnight.

THREE. Right. [*Resumes crocheting.*] Now, what else do you want?

EIGHT. It doesn't seem to fit.

FOUR. The boy's whole story is flimsy. He claimed he was at the movies. That's a little ridiculous, isn't it? He couldn't even remember what picture he saw.

THREE. That's right. Did you hear that? [*To* FOUR.] You're absolutely right.

FIVE. He didn't have any ticket stub.

EIGHT. Who keeps a ticket stub at the movies?

FOUR [*to* FIVE]. That's true enough.

FIVE. I suppose. But the cashier didn't remember him.

THREE. And the ticket taker didn't, either.

TEN. Look—what about the woman across the street? If her testimony don't prove it, then nothing can.

TWELVE. That's right. She saw the killing, didn't she?

FOREMAN [*rapping on table*]. Ladies! Let's go in order.

TEN [*loudly*]. Just a minute. Here's a woman who's lying in bed and can't sleep. It's hot, you know. [*Gets up and begins to walk around, blowing her nose and talking.*] Anyway, she wakes up and she looks out the window, and right across the street she sees the boy knife his father.

EIGHT. How can she really be sure it was the boy when she saw it through the windows of a passing elevated train?

TEN. She's known him all his life. His window is right opposite hers—across the el tracks. [*Impressively.*] She swore she saw him do it!

EIGHT. I heard her swear to it.

TEN. Okay. And they proved in court that you can look through the windows of a passing el train at night, and see what's happening on the other side. They proved it.

EIGHT. Weren't you telling us just a minute or two ago that you can't trust *them?* That you can't believe *them?*

TEN [*coldly*]. So?

EIGHT. Then I'd like to ask you something. How come you believed *her?* She's one of *them,* too, isn't she? [TEN *crosses up to* EIGHT.]

TEN. You're a pretty smart cookie, aren't you?

FOREMAN [*rising*]. Now, take it easy. [THREE *gets up and goes to* TEN.]

THREE. Come on. Sit down. [*Leads* TEN *back to her seat.*] What're you letting her get you all upset for? Relax. [TEN *and* THREE *sit down.*]

FOUR. Ladies, they did take us out to that woman's room and we looked through the windows of a passing el train—[*To* EIGHT.]—didn't we?

EIGHT [*nodding*]. Yes. We looked.

FOUR. And weren't you able to see what happened on the other side?

EIGHT. I didn't see as well as they told me I would, but I did see what happened on the other side.

TEN [*snapping at* EIGHT]. You see! You *do* see, don't you?

FOREMAN [*sitting again*]. Let's calm down now. [*To* FIVE.] It's your turn.

FIVE. I'll pass it.

FOREMAN. That's your privilege. [*To* SIX.] How about you?

SIX [*slowly*]. I don't know. What convinced me was the testimony of those people across the hall. Didn't they say something about an argument between the father and the boy around seven o'clock that night? I mean—I can be wrong.

ELEVEN. I think it was eight o'clock. Not seven.

EIGHT [*glancing at some notes she has before her*]. That's right. Eight o'clock.

FOUR. They heard the father hit the boy twice and then saw the boy walk angrily out of the house.

SIX. Right.

EIGHT. What does that prove?

SIX. Well, it doesn't exactly prove anything. It's just part of the picture. I didn't say it proved anything.

FOREMAN. Anything else?

SIX. No. [*Rises and goes to water cooler for a drink and then sits again after getting it.*]

SEVEN. I don't know—most of it's been said already. We can

talk all day about this thing, but I think we're wasting our time.

EIGHT. I don't.

FOUR. Neither do I. Go on.

SEVEN. Look at the boy's record. He stole a car. He's been arrested for mugging. [*The women all stiffen at this point.*] I think they said he once stabbed somebody in the arm.

FOUR. They did.

SEVEN. He was picked up for knife fighting. At fifteen he was in a reform school.

THREE [*crocheting swiftly*]. And they sent him to reform school for stabbing someone.

SEVEN [*scornfully*]. This is a very fine boy!

EIGHT. Ever since he was five years old his father beat him up regularly. He used his fists.

SEVEN. So would I—on a boy like that! Or if I couldn't—I'd see that his father did!

THREE [*slamming down her crocheting*]. You're right. It's the kids nowadays. The way they are—you know? They don't listen. [*Bitterly.*] I've got a boy. When he was eight years old, I caught him with some of the neighborhood gang—fighting—and out in the street! After all I'd said about staying away from those toughs—he goes and joins them! I gave him a whipping he wouldn't forget! And you know what? When he was fifteen, he hit me—a woman—his own mother—in the face! He's big, you know. I haven't seen him in three years. Maybe I'm better off. A rotten kid! I hate tough kids! You work your heart out. . . . [*Pauses.*] All right. Let's get on with it. . . . [*Gets up and goes to window, very embarrassed.*]

FOUR. We're missing the point here. This boy—let's admit he's a product of a filthy neighborhood and a broken home. We can't help that. We're not here to go into the reasons why slums are breeding grounds for criminals; they are. I know it. So do you. The children who come out of slum backgrounds are potential menaces to society.

TEN. You said it there. I don't want any part of them, believe me. [*There is dead silence for a moment, and then* FIVE *speaks haltingly.*]

FIVE. I've lived in a slum all my life.

TEN. Now, wait a minute.

FIVE. I used to play in a backyard that was filled with garbage. Maybe it still smells on me.

FOREMAN. Now, let's be reasonable. There's nothing personal. . . .

FIVE [*rising, slamming her hand down on the table*]. There *is* something personal! [*Then she catches herself, and seeing everyone looking at her, sits down, fists clenched.*]

THREE [*turning from window*]. Come on, now. She didn't mean you. Let's not be so sensitive. [*There is a long pause.*]

EIGHT [*breaking silence*]. Whom did she mean?

ELEVEN. I can understand this sensitivity.

FOREMAN. Now, let's stop the bickering.

TWELVE. We're wasting time.

FOREMAN [*to* EIGHT]. It's your turn.

EIGHT. All right. I had a peculiar feeling about this trial. Somehow I felt that the defense counsel never really conducted a thorough cross-examination. Too many questions were left unasked.

FOUR. While it doesn't change my opinion about the guilt of the boy, still, I agree with you that the defense counsel was bad.

THREE [*crocheting rapidly and not looking up*]. So-o-o-o?

EIGHT. This is a point.

THREE. What about facts?

EIGHT. So many questions were never answered.

THREE [*annoyed*]. What about the questions that were answered? For instance, let's talk about that cute little switch knife. You know, the one that fine, upright boy admitted buying.

EIGHT. All right, let's talk about it. Let's get it in here and look at it. I'd like to see it again, Madam Foreman. [FOREMAN *looks at her questioningly and then gets up and goes to door* L.]

[*During the following dialogue the* FOREMAN *knocks. The* GUARD *unlocks the door and comes in* L. *The* FOREMAN *whispers to her; the* GUARD *nods and leaves, locking the door. The* FOREMAN *returns to her seat.*]

THREE. We saw the thing once. I don't see why we have to look at it again. [*To* FOUR.] What do you think?

FOUR. The lady has a right to see exhibits in evidence.

THREE [*shrugging*]. Okay with me.

FOUR [*to* EIGHT]. This knife is a pretty strong piece of evidence, don't you agree?

EIGHT. I do.

FOUR. Now, let's get the sequence of events right as they relate to the switch knife.

TWELVE. The boy admits going out of his house at eight o'clock, after being slapped by his father.

EIGHT. Or punched.

FOUR. Or punched. [*Gets up and begins to pace at* R *stage, moving* D R *to* U R *and back again.*] He went to a neighborhood store and bought a switch knife. The storekeeper was arrested the following day when he admitted selling it to the boy.

THREE. I think everyone agrees that it's an unusual knife. Pretty hard to forget something like that.

FOUR. The storekeeper identified the knife and said it was the only one of its kind he had in stock. Why did the boy get it?

SEVEN [*sarcastically*]. As a present for a friend of his, he says.

FOUR [*pausing in her pacing*]. Am I right so far?

EIGHT. Right.

THREE. You bet she's right. [*To* ALL.] Now, listen to this lady. She knows what she's talking about.

FOUR [*standing at* R *stage*]. Next, the boy claims that on the way home the knife must have fallen through a hole in his coat pocket, says he never saw it again. Now there's a story, ladies. You know what actually happened. The boy took the knife home, and a few hours later stabbed his father with it and even remembered to wipe off the fingerprints.

[*The door* L *opens and the* GUARD *walks in with an oddly de-signed knife with a tag on it.* FOUR *crosses* L *and takes the knife from her. The* GUARD *goes out* L, *closing and locking the door.*]

FOUR [*at* L C, *holding up knife*]. Everyone connected with the case identified this knife. Now, are you trying to tell me that someone picked it up off the street and went up to the boy's house and stabbed his father with it just to be amusing?

EIGHT. No. I'm saying that it's possible that the boy lost the knife, and that someone else stabbed his father with a similar knife. It's possible. [FOUR *flips the knife open and jams it into the wall, just downstage of door* L. *The women are, in general, a bit startled at the gesture.*]

FOUR [*standing back to allow others to see*]. Take a look at that knife. It's a very strange knife. I've never seen one like it before in my life. Neither had the storekeeper who sold it. [EIGHT *reaches casually into her purse and withdraws an object. No one notices her. She stands up.*] Aren't you trying to make us accept a pretty incredible coincidence?

EIGHT [*moving toward* FOUR]. I'm not trying to make anyone accept it. I'm just saying it's possible.

THREE [*rising, shouting*]. And I'm saying it's not possible. [EIGHT *swiftly flicks open blade of a switch knife and jams it into wall next to first knife. They are exactly alike. There are several gasps and a scream. Everyone stares at knife. There is a long silence.* THREE *continues, slowly, amazed.*] What are you trying to do?

TEN [*loudly*]. Yeah, what is this? Who do you think you are?

FIVE. Look at it! It's the same knife!

FOREMAN. Quiet! Let's be quiet. [*They quiet down.* THREE *sits again.*]

FOUR. Where did you get it?

EIGHT. I got it in a little junk shop around the corner from the boy's house. It cost two dollars.

THREE. Now, listen to me!

EIGHT. I'm listening.

THREE. You pulled a real smart trick here, but you proved absolutely zero. Maybe there are ten knives like that. So what?

EIGHT. Maybe there are.

THREE. The boy lied, and you know it.

EIGHT [*crossing back to her seat, sitting*]. And maybe he didn't lie. Maybe he did lose the knife and maybe he did go to the movies. Maybe the reason the cashier didn't see him was because he sneaked into the movies and maybe he was ashamed to say so. [*Looks around.*] Is there anybody here who didn't sneak into the movies once or twice when they were young? [*There is a long silence.*]

ELEVEN. I didn't.

FOUR. Really, not even once?

ELEVEN. We didn't have movies.

FOUR. Oh. [*Crosses back to her place and sits.*]

EIGHT. Maybe he did go to the movies, maybe he didn't. And —he may have lied. [*To* TEN.] Do you think he lied?

TEN [*violently*]. Now, that's a stupid question. Sure, he lied!

EIGHT [*to* FOUR]. Do you?

FOUR. You don't have to ask me that. You know my answer. He lied.

EIGHT [*to* FIVE]. Do you think he lied? [FIVE *can't answer immediately. She looks around nervously.*]

FIVE. I—I don't know.

SEVEN. Now, wait a second. What are you, the boy's lawyer? Listen, there are still eleven of us who think he's guilty. You're alone. What do you think you're going to accomplish? If you want to be stubborn and hang this jury, he'll be tried again and found guilty, sure as he's born.

EIGHT. You're probably right.

SEVEN. So, what are you going to do about it? We can be here all night.

NINE. It's only one night. A man may die.

SEVEN. Oh, now. Come on.

EIGHT [*to* NINE]. Well, yes, that's true.

FOREMAN. I think we ought to get on with it now.

THREE. Right. Let's get going here.

TEN [*to* THREE]. How do you like this woman? [THREE *shrugs and turns to* EIGHT.]

THREE. Well, what do you say? You're the one holding up the show.

FOUR [*to* EIGHT]. Obviously you don't think the boy is guilty.

EIGHT. I have a doubt in my mind.

FOUR. But you haven't really presented anything to us that makes it possible for us to understand your doubt. There's the old man downstairs. He heard it. He heard the boy shriek it out. . . .

THREE. The woman across the el tracks, she saw it!

SEVEN. We know he bought a switch knife that night and we don't know where he really was. At the movies?

FOREMAN. Earlier that night the boy and his father did have a fight.

FOUR. He's been a violent boy all the way, and while that doesn't prove anything . . .

TEN. Still, you know. . . .

EIGHT [*standing*]. I've got a proposition to make. [FIVE *stands and puts her hands on back of her chair. Several jurors glare at her. She sinks her head down a bit, then sits down.*] I want to call for a vote. I want the eleven of you to vote by secret ballot. I'll abstain. If there are still eleven votes for guilty, I won't stand alone. We'll take in a guilty verdict right now.

SEVEN. Okay. Let's do it.

FOREMAN. That sounds fair. Is everyone agreed?

FOUR. I certainly am.

TWELVE. Let's do it.

ELEVEN [*slowly*]. Perhaps this is best. [EIGHT *walks over to the window and stands there for a moment looking out, then turns as the* FOREMAN *passes ballot slips to all of them.* EIGHT *tenses as* JURORS *begin to write. Then folded ballots are passed back to* FOREMAN. *She flips through the folded ballots, counts them to be sure she has eleven, and then begins to open them, reading the verdict each time.*]

FOREMAN. Guilty. Guilty. Guilty. Guilty. Guilty. Guilty.

THREE. That's six.

FOREMAN. Please. [*Fumbles with one ballot.*] Six guilty. Guilty. Guilty. Guilty. [*Pauses for a moment at the tenth ballot and then reads.*] Not guilty. [THREE *slams her hand down hard on the table.* EIGHT *starts for the table.*] Guilty.

TEN [*angrily*]. How do you like that!

SEVEN [*standing, outraged, and stamping her foot*]. Who was it? I think we have a right to know. [*Looks about. No one moves.*]

CURTAIN

ACT TWO

AT RISE OF CURTAIN: *It is only a second or two later. The* JURORS *are in the same positions as they were at the end of Act One.*]

THREE [*slamming down her crocheting*]. All right! Who did it? What idiot changed her vote?

EIGHT. Is that the way to talk about a man's life?[*Sits at her place again.*]

THREE. Whose life are you talking about? The life of the dead man or the life of a murderer?

SEVEN. I want to know. Who?

THREE. So do I.

ELEVEN. Excuse me. This was a secret ballot.

THREE. No one looked while we did it, but now I want to know.

ELEVEN. A secret ballot; we agreed on that point, no? If the lady wants it to remain a secret . . .

THREE [*standing up angrily*]. What do you mean? There are no secrets in here! I know who it was. [*Turns to* FIVE.] What's the matter with you? You come in here and you vote guilty and then this slick—[*Nods toward* EIGHT.]—cookie starts to tear your heart out with stories about a poor little boy who just couldn't help becoming a murderer. So you change your vote. If that isn't the most sickening . . . [FIVE *edges her chair away from* THREE *and continues knitting.*]

FOREMAN. Now, hold it. [SEVEN *sits again, slowly.*]

FOUR [*to* THREE]. I agree with you that the boy is guilty, but let's be fair.

THREE. Hold it? Be fair? That's just what I'm saying. We're

28

trying to put a guilty man into the chair where he belongs—
and all of a sudden we're paying attention to fairy tales.
[*Crochets indignantly.*]

FIVE. Now, just a minute——

THREE [*bending toward* FIVE, *wagging finger at her*]. Now,
you listen to me——

FOREMAN [*rapping on table*]. Let's try to keep this organized,
ladies.

FOUR. It isn't organized, but let's try to be civilized.

ELEVEN. Please. I would like to say something here. I have
always thought that a person was entitled to have unpopular
opinions in this country. That is the reason I came here. I
wanted to have the right to disagree.

THREE. Do you disagree with us?

ELEVEN. Usually, I would. In this one case I agree with you,
but the point I wish to make is that in my own country, I
am ashamed to say——

TEN. Oh, now-w-w, what do we have to listen to—the whole
history of your country? [THREE *sits again in disgust.*]

FOUR. It's always wise to bear in mind what has happened in
other countries, when people aren't allowed to disagree; but
we are, so let's stick to the subject.

SEVEN. Yes, let's stick to the subject. [*To* FIVE.] I want to
ask you, what made you change your vote?

THREE. I want to know, too. You haven't told us yet.

FIVE. Why do you think I did change my vote? [*Her lips move
as she counts her stitches.*]

SEVEN. Because I do. Now get on with it.

NINE [*quietly*]. There's nothing for her to tell you. She didn't
change her vote. I did. [ALL *look at* NINE.]

FIVE [*to* THREE]. I was going to tell you, but you were so sure
of yourself.

THREE. Sorry. [*To* NINE.] Okay, now. . . .

NINE. Maybe you'd like to know why.

THREE [*not giving her a chance*]. Let me tell you why that
boy's a——

FOREMAN. The lady wants to talk. [THREE *subsides.*]

NINE [*to* FOREMAN]. Thank you. [*Points at* EIGHT.] This lady chose not to stand alone against us. That's her right. It takes a great deal of courage to stand alone even if you believe in something very strongly. She left the verdict up to us. She gambled for support, and I gave it to her. I want to hear more. The vote is ten to two. [JURORS TWO *and* FOUR *get up at about the same instant and walk to the water cooler as* TEN *speaks.*]

TEN. That's fine. If the speech is over, let's go on. [FOREMAN *gets up, goes to door* L, *pulls tagged knife from wall and then knocks on door. The door is opened by the* GUARD. FOREMAN *hands* GUARD *the tagged switch knife.* GUARD *goes out, and* FOREMAN *takes other switch knife and puts it in the middle of the table. She sits again. The other* JURORS *talk on, in pantomime, as* TWO *and* FOUR *stand by the water cooler.*]

FOUR [*filling cup*]. If there was anything in the boy's favor, I'd vote not guilty.

TWO. I don't see what it is.

FOUR [*handing cup to* TWO, *then drawing drink for herself*]. Neither do I. They're clutching at straws.

TWO. As guilty as they get—that's the boy, I suppose.

FOUR. It's that one juror that's holding out, but she'll come around. She's got to and, fundamentally, she's a very reasonable person.

TWO. I guess so.

FOUR. They haven't come up with one real fact yet to back up a not guilty verdict.

TWO. It's hard, you know.

FOUR. Yes, it is. And what does "guilty beyond a reasonable doubt" really mean?

TWO. What's a "reasonable doubt"?

FOUR. Exactly. When a life is at stake, what is a reasonable doubt? You've got to have law and order; you've got to draw the line somewhere; if you don't, everyone would start knifing people.

TWO. Not much doubt here.

FOUR. Two women think so. I wonder why. I really wonder why.

TWO. You do hear stories about innocent men who have gone to jail—or death, sometimes—then years later things turn up.

FOUR. And then on the other hand some killers get turned loose and they go and do it again. They squeeze out on some technicality and kill again. [*Throws her cup into the wastebasket, walks back and sits. We then hear* THREE *say to* FIVE.]

THREE. Look, hon', now that we've kind of cooled off, why— ah—I was a little excited a minute ago. Well, you know how it is—I didn't mean to get nasty. Nothing personal. [TWO *trails back to her place and sits again.*]

FIVE [*after staring at* THREE *for a moment, speaking coldly*]. Think nothing of it.

SEVEN [*to* EIGHT]. Look, supposing you answer me this. If the boy didn't kill him, who did?

EIGHT. As far as I know, we're supposed to decide whether or not the boy on trial is guilty. We're not concerned with anyone else's motives here.

SEVEN. I suppose, but who else had a motive?

EIGHT. The boy's father was along in years; maybe an old grudge.

NINE. Remember, it is "guilty beyond a reasonable doubt." This is an important thing to remember.

THREE [*to* TEN]. Everyone's a lawyer. [*To* NINE.] Supposing you explain to us what your reasonable doubts are.

NINE. This is not easy. So far, it's only a feeling I have. A feeling. Perhaps you don't understand.

THREE [*abruptly*]. No. I don't.

TEN. A feeling! What are we going to do, spend the night talking about your feelings? What about the facts?

THREE. You took the words right out of my mouth. [*To* NINE.] Look, the old man heard the boy yell, "I'm gonna kill you." A second later he heard the father's body falling, and he saw the boy running out of the house fifteen seconds after that.

SEVEN. Where's the reasonable doubt in that?

TWELVE. That's right. And let's not forget the woman across the street. She looked into the open window and saw the boy stab his father. She saw it!

THREE. Now, if that's not enough for you——

EIGHT [*quietly firm*]. It's not enough for me.

FOUR. What *is* enough for you? I'd like to know.

SEVEN. How do you like her? It's like talking into a dead 'phone.

FOUR. The woman saw the killing through the windows of a moving elevated train. The train had five cars and she saw it through the windows of the last two cars. She remembers the most insignificant details.

THREE. Well, what have you got to say about that?

EIGHT. I don't know. It doesn't sound right to me.

THREE. Well, supposing you think about it. [*To* TWELVE.] Want to see the pattern for a crocheted skirt my daughter sent me? [TWELVE *nods. They put their heads together over pattern.*] It doesn't look very hard.

TWELVE. Wouldn't it be out of style by the time you got it done?

EIGHT. This isn't a sewing circle. [*Rises and snatches pattern away.* THREE *jumps up.*]

THREE. Now, wait a minute!

EIGHT. This is a man's life.

THREE [*angrily*]. Who do you think you are?

SEVEN [*rising*]. All right, let's take it easy. [EIGHT *sits again.*]

THREE. I've got a good mind to walk around this table and slap her!

FOREMAN. Now, please. I don't want any fights in here.

THREE. Did you see her? The nerve! The absolute nerve!

TEN. All right. Forget it. It don't mean anything.

SIX. How about sitting down?

THREE. "This isn't a sewing circle." Who does she think she is? [SIX *and* TEN *urge* THREE *back into her seat.* SEVEN *sits again, and* ALL *are seated once more.*]

FOUR [*when quiet is restored*]. Weren't we talking about elevated trains?

EIGHT. Yes, we were.

FOUR. So?

EIGHT. All right. How long does it take an elevated train going at top speed to pass a given point?

FOUR. What has that got to do with anything?

EIGHT. How long would it take? Guess.

FOUR. I wouldn't have the slightest idea.

SEVEN. Neither would I.

NINE. Nobody mentioned it.

EIGHT [*to* FIVE]. What do you think?

FIVE. About ten or twelve seconds—maybe.

EIGHT. I'd say that was a fair guess. Anyone else?

ELEVEN. I would think about ten seconds, perhaps. . . .

TWO [*reflectively*]. About ten seconds, yes.

FOUR. All right, we're agreed. Ten seconds. [*To* EIGHT.] What are you getting at?

EIGHT. This. An el train passes a given point in ten seconds. That given point is the window of the room in which the killing took place. You can almost reach out of the window of that room and touch the el. Right?

FOREMAN. That's right. I tried it.

FOUR. So?

EIGHT. All right. Now let me ask you this. Did anyone here ever live right next to the el tracks?

FIVE. I've lived close to them.

EIGHT. They make a lot of noise, don't they? [FIVE *nods.*] I've lived right by the el tracks. When your window is open, and the train goes by, the noise is almost unbearable. You can't hear yourself think.

TEN [*impatiently*]. You can't hear yourself think. Get to the point.

EIGHT. The old man who lived downstairs heard the boy say——

THREE [*interrupting*]. He didn't *say* it, he screamed it.

EIGHT. The old man heard the boy scream, "I'm going to kill

you," and one second later he heard a body fall. One second. That's the testimony, right?

TWO. Right.

EIGHT. The woman across the street looked through the windows of the last two cars of the el and saw the body fall. Right?

FOUR. Right.

TWELVE. So?

EIGHT [*slowly*]. The last two cars. [*Slight pause, then repeats.*] The last two cars.

TEN. What are you giving us here?

EIGHT. An el train takes ten seconds to pass a given point, or two seconds per car. That el had been going by the old man's window for at least six seconds and maybe more *before the body fell,* according to the woman. The old man would have had to hear the boy say, "I'm going to kill you," while the front of the el was roaring past his nose. It's not possible that he could have heard it.

THREE. What do you mean! Sure, he could have heard it.

EIGHT. With an el train going by?

THREE. He said the boy yelled it out.

EIGHT. An el train makes a lot of noise.

THREE. It's enough for me.

FOUR. It's enough for me, too.

NINE. I don't think he could have heard it.

TWO. Maybe the old man didn't hear it. I mean with the el noise. . . .

THREE. What are you people talking about? Are you calling the old man a liar?

EIGHT [*shaking her head*]. Something doesn't fit.

FIVE. Well, it stands to reason——

THREE. You're crazy. Why would he lie? What's he got to gain?

NINE. Attention. . . . Maybe.

THREE. You keep coming up with these bright sayings. Why don't you send one in to a newspaper? They pay two dollars.

EIGHT [*hard, to* THREE]. What does that have to do with a

man's life? [*Then, to* NINE.] Why might the old man have
lied? You have a right to be heard.

NINE [*after moment's hesitation*]. It's just that I looked at
him for a very long time. The seam of his jacket was split
under the arm. Did you notice that? He was a very old man
with a torn jacket, and he carried two canes. [*Gets up,
moves* R *and leans against wall.*] I think I know him better
than anyone here. This is a quiet, frightened, insignificant
man who has been nothing all his life—who has never had
recognition—his name in the newspapers. Nobody knows
him after seventy-five years. This is a very sad thing. A man
like this needs to be recognized—to be questioned, and
listened to, and quoted just once. This is very important. . . .

TWELVE. And you're trying to tell us he lied about a thing
like this just so he could be important?

NINE. No, he wouldn't really lie. But perhaps he'd make himself believe that he heard those words and recognized the
boy's face.

THREE. Well—[*Loud and brassy.*]—that's the most fantastic
story I've ever heard. How can you make up a thing like
that?

NINE [*doggedly*]. I'm not making it up.

THREE. You must be making it up. People don't lie about
things like that.

NINE. He made himself believe he told the truth.

THREE. What do you know about it?

NINE [*low but firm*]. I speak from experience. [*There is a
long pause.*]

FOREMAN [*to* EIGHT]. All right. Is there anything else? [TWO
holds up a box of cough drops and speaks to FOREMAN.]

TWO. Cough drop?

FOREMAN [*waving it aside*]. No, thank you.

TWO [*hesitantly*]. Anybody—want a cough—drop? [*Offers
box around.*]

FOREMAN [*sharply*]. Come on. Let's get on with it.

EIGHT. I'll take one. [TWO *hands her box.*] Thank you. [*Takes one and returns box.*] Now—there's something else I'd like to point out here. I think we proved that the old man couldn't have heard the boy say, "I'm going to kill you."

THREE. Well, I disagree.

FOUR [*to* THREE]. Let's hear her through, anyway.

EIGHT. But supposing the old man really did hear the boy say, "I'm going to kill you." This phrase—how many times has each of you used it? Probably hundreds. "If you do that once more, Junior, I'm going to murder you." Or your husband yells, "Come on, Rocky, kill him!" We say it every day. This doesn't mean that we're really going to kill someone.

FOUR. Don't the circumstances alter that somewhat?

TWELVE. The old man was murdered.

THREE. One thing more. The phrase was "I'm going to kill you." And the kid screamed it out at the top of his lungs.

FOUR. That's the way I understand it.

THREE. Now don't try and tell me he didn't mean it. Anybody says a thing like that the way he said it—they mean it.

TEN. And how they mean it!

EIGHT. Well, let me ask you this. Do you really think the boy would shout out a thing like that so the whole neighborhood would hear it? I don't think so. He's much too bright for that.

TEN [*exploding*]. Bright! He's a common, ignorant slob. He don't even speak good English!

ELEVEN [*slowly*]. He *doesn't* even speak good English.

FOUR. The boy is clever enough. [FOUR'S *line is spoken as* TEN *rises and glowers at* ELEVEN. *There is a momentary pause.* TEN *sits again as* FIVE *gets up and looks around. She is nervous.*]

FIVE. I'd like to change my vote to not guilty. [THREE *slams her crocheting onto the table, then walks to the window.*]

FOREMAN. Are you sure?

FIVE. Yes. I'm sure.

FOREMAN. The vote is nine to three in favor of guilty.

FOUR [*to* FIVE]. I'd like to know why you've changed your vote.

FIVE. I think there's a doubt.

THREE [*turning abruptly from window, shouting*]. Where? What is the doubt?

FIVE. There's the knife. . . .

SEVEN [*slamming her hand down on the table*]. Oh, fine!

TEN. She—[*Motions at* EIGHT.]—she talked you into believing a fairy tale.

FOUR [*to* FIVE]. Go on. Give us the reasons.

FIVE. The old man, too. Maybe he didn't lie, but then just *maybe* he did. Maybe the old man doesn't like the boy.

SEVEN. Well, if that isn't the end.

FIVE. I believe there is a reasonable doubt. [*Sits again.*]

SEVEN. What are you basing it on? Stories that this woman— [*Indicates* EIGHT.]—made up! She ought to write for Amazing Detective Monthly. She'd make a fortune. Listen, the boy had a lawyer, didn't he? Why didn't his lawyer bring up all these points?

FIVE. Lawyers can't think of everything.

SEVEN. Oh, heavens! [*To* EIGHT.] You sit in here and pull stories out of thin air. Now we're supposed to believe that the old man didn't get out of bed, run to the door and see the boy running downstairs fifteen seconds after the killing.

FOUR. That's the testimony, I believe.

SEVEN. And the old man swore to this—yes—he swore to this only so he could be important. [*Looks over at* NINE.]

FIVE. Did the old man say he *ran* to the door?

SEVEN. Ran. Walked. What's the difference? He got there.

FIVE. I don't remember what he *said*. But I don't see how he could *run*.

FOUR. He said he *went*. I remember it now. He *went* from his bedroom to the front door. That's enough, isn't it?

EIGHT. Where was his bedroom, again?

TEN [*disinterestedly*]. Down the hall somewhere.

EIGHT [*angrily*]. Down the hall! Are we to send a man off to die because it's down the hall *somewhere?*

TEN. I thought you remembered everything. Don't you remember that?

EIGHT. No, I don't.

NINE. I don't remember, either.

EIGHT. Madam Foreman, I'd like to take a look at the diagram of the apartment.

SEVEN. Why don't we have them run the trial over just so you can get everything straight?

EIGHT. The bedroom is down the hall somewhere. Do you *know*—do you know exactly where it is? Please. A boy's life is at stake. Do you *know?*

SEVEN. Well, ah . . .

EIGHT. Madam Foreman.

FOREMAN [*rising*]. I heard you. [*Goes to door* L *and knocks.*]

[*During the ensuing dialogue the* GUARD *opens door* L. *The* FOREMAN *whispers to her. The* GUARD *nods, then closes door.*]

THREE [*stepping away from window, moving a few steps toward* EIGHT]. All right. What's this one for? How come you're the only one in the room who wants to see exhibits all the time?

FIVE. I want to see this one, too.

NINE. So do I.

THREE. And I want to stop wasting time. [*Returns to table, sits and resumes her crocheting.*]

FOUR. Are we going to start wading through all that nonsense about where the body was found?

EIGHT. We're not. We're going to find out how a man who's had two strokes in the past three years, and who walks with a pair of canes, could get to his front door in fifteen seconds.

THREE. He said twenty seconds.

TWO. He said fifteen.

THREE. How does he know how long fifteen seconds is? You can't judge that kind of thing.

NINE. He said fifteen. He was very positive about it.

THREE [*angrily*]. He's an old man. You saw that. Half the

time he was confused. How could he be positive about—anything? [*Looks around sheepishly, unable to cover her blunder.*] Well, ah—you know.

EIGHT. No, I don't know. Maybe you know.

[*Door* L *opens and the* GUARD *walks in carrying a large pen-and-ink diagram of the apartment done on heavy drawing board stock. It is a railroad flat. A bedroom faces the el tracks. Behind it is a series of rooms off a long hall. In the front bedroom there is a mark where the body was found. At the back of the apartment is the entrance into the apartment hall from the building hall. There is a flight of stairs in the building hall. The diagram is clearly labeled, and included in the information on it are the dimensions of the various rooms. The* GUARD *gives the diagram to the* FOREMAN, *who has remained by door* L.]

GUARD. Is this what you wanted?

FOREMAN. That's right. Thank you.

GUARD. Sure, that's my job. [*Nods and goes out* L, *closing and locking door as she goes.* EIGHT *rises and starts toward* FOREMAN.]

FOREMAN. You want this?

EIGHT. Yes, please. [FOREMAN *nods.* EIGHT *takes diagram and crosses* U R, *takes chair from* U R *corner and brings it* R C, *half facing table. She sets diagram up on chair so all can see it.* EIGHT *looks it over. Several* JURORS *get up to see it better.* THREE, TEN *and* SEVEN, *however, barely bother to look at it.* THREE *sits abruptly again at table.*]

SEVEN [*to* TEN]. Do me a favor. [*Slumps in chair.*] Wake me up when this is over.

TEN. I looked at that diagram for two hours; enough is enough.

FOUR. Some of us are interested. Go ahead.

EIGHT. All right. This is the apartment in which the killing took place. The old man's apartment is directly beneath it, and exactly the same. [*Points.*] Here are the el tracks. The bedroom. Another bedroom. Living room. Bathroom.

Kitchen. And this is the hall. Here's the front door to the apartment, and here are the steps. [*Points to front bedroom, then to front door.*] Now, the old man was in bed in this room. He says he got up, went out into the hall, down the hall to the front door, and opened it and looked out just in time to see the boy racing down the stairs. Am I right?

FOUR. That's the story.

SEVEN. That's what happened!

EIGHT. Fifteen seconds after he heard the body fall.

ELEVEN. Correct. [FOREMAN *and other* JURORS *who have come to look at diagram now drift back to table and sit again.*]

EIGHT [*still by diagram at* R C]. His bed was at the window. [*Peers at diagram.*] It's twelve feet from his bed to the bedroom door. The length of the hall is forty-three feet six inches. He had to get up out of bed, get his canes, walk twelve feet, open the bedroom door, walk forty-three feet and open the front door—all in fifteen seconds. Do you think this possible?

TEN. You know it's possible.

FOUR. I don't see why not.

THREE. He would have been in a hurry. He did hear the scream.

ELEVEN. He can only walk very slowly. They had to help him into the witness chair.

THREE. You make it sound like a long walk. It's not. [EIGHT *goes* D L *and takes two chairs. She crosses* D R, *near water cooler, and puts them together to indicate a bed.*]

NINE. For an old man who uses canes, it's a long walk.

THREE [*to* EIGHT]. What are you doing?

EIGHT. I want to try this thing. Let's see how long it took him. I'm going to pace off twelve feet—the length of the bedroom. [*Begins to do so, pacing from* D R, *across the stage, toward* D C.]

THREE. You're crazy. You can't re-create a thing like that.

ELEVEN. Perhaps if we could see it—this is an important point.

THREE [*angrily*]. It's a ridiculous waste of time!

SIX. Let her do it.

FOUR. I can't see any harm in it. Foolish, but go ahead.

EIGHT. Hand me a chair, please. [NINE *pushes chair from right end of table to* EIGHT *and then sits again.*] All right. [*Places chair at point she has paced off.*] This is the bedroom door. How far would you say it is from here to the door of this room?

SIX [*as* ALL *look*]. I'd say it was twenty feet. [*Several* JURORS, *excluding* THREE, SEVEN *and* TEN, *rise and stand near their places, watching.*]

TWO. Just about.

EIGHT. Twenty feet is close enough. All right, from here to the door and back is about forty feet. It's shorter than the length of the hall the old man had to move through. Wouldn't you say that?

NINE. A few feet, maybe.

TEN. Look, this is absolutely insane. What makes you think you can do this?

FOREMAN. We can't stop her.

EIGHT. Do you mind if I try it? According to you, it'll only take fifteen seconds. We can spare that. [*Walks over to two chairs and lies down on them.*] Who's got a watch with a second hand?

TWO. I have. [*Indicates wrist watch.*]

EIGHT. When you want me to start, stamp your foot. That'll be the body falling.

TWO. We'll time you from there.

EIGHT [*lying down on two chairs*]. Let's say he keeps his canes right at his bedside. Right?

FOUR. Right!

EIGHT. Okay. I'm ready.

TWO [*explaining*]. I'm waiting for the hand to get to sixty. [ALL *watch carefully; then,* TWO *stamps her foot, loudly.* EIGHT *begins to get up. Slowly she swings her legs over edges of chairs, reaches for imaginary canes and struggles to her feet.* TWO *stares at her watch.* EIGHT *now walks as a crippled old man would walk. She goes toward chair which is serving as bedroom door. She reaches it and pretends to open it.*]

TEN [*shouting*]. Speed it up. He walked twice as fast as that. [EIGHT, *not having stopped for this outburst, begins to walk simulated forty-foot hallway to door* L *and back to chair.*]

ELEVEN. This is, I think, even more quickly than the old man walked in the courtroom.

THREE. No, it isn't.

EIGHT. If you think I should go faster, I will.

FOUR. Speed it up a little. [EIGHT *speeds up her pace slightly. She reaches door* L *and turns now, heading back, hobbling as an old man would hobble, bent over the imaginary canes.* ALL *watch her tensely. She hobbles back to chair, which also serves as the front door. She stops there and pretends to unlock door. Then she pretends to push it open.*]

EIGHT [*loudly*]. Stop.

TWO [*eyes glued to watch*]. Right.

EIGHT. What's the time?

TWO. Fifteen—twenty—thirty—thirty-five—thirty-nine seconds, exactly. [*Moves toward* EIGHT. *Other* JURORS *now move in toward* EIGHT *also.*]

THREE. That can't be!

ELEVEN. Thirty-nine seconds!

FOUR. Now, that's interesting.

SEVEN [*looking at* JURORS]. Say, now—you know. . . .

NINE. What do you think of that!

ELEVEN [*nodding*]. Thirty-nine seconds. Thirty-nine.

FOUR. And the old man swore, on his oath, that it was fifteen.

ELEVEN [*pointing to* EIGHT]. He may have been a little bit off on the speed that the old man moved at—but twenty-four seconds off . . . well, now, you know. . . .

FOREMAN. Far be it from me to call anyone a liar, but even allowing for quite a difference in speed between the old

man and you—[*Motions at* EIGHT.]—why, still, there's
quite a——

FOUR. Quite a discrepancy.

EIGHT. It's my guess that the old man was trying to get to the
door, heard someone racing down the stairs and *assumed*
that it was the boy.

SIX. I think that's possible.

THREE [*infuriated*]. Assumed? Now, listen to me, everyone.
I've seen all kinds of dishonesty in my day—but this little
display takes the cake.

EIGHT. What dishonesty?

THREE [*to* FOUR]. Tell her! [FOUR *turns away* D R *and sits
silently in one of the two chairs there.* THREE *looks at her
and then strides to* EIGHT.] You come in here with your
heart bleeding all over the floor about slums and injustice
and you make up these wild stories, and you've got a couple
of soft-hearted sob sisters listening to you. Well, I'm not.
I'm sick of it all. [*To* ALL.] What's the matter with you
people? This boy is guilty! He's got to burn! We're letting
him slip through our fingers. . . .

EIGHT [*calmly*]. Our fingers? Are you his executioner?

THREE [*raging*]. I'm one of 'em!

EIGHT. Perhaps you'd like to pull the switch.

THREE [*shouting*]. For this good-for-nothing? You bet I'd like
to pull the switch!

EIGHT [*shaking her head sadly*]. I'm sorry for you.

THREE [*shouting*]. Don't start with me!

EIGHT. What it must feel like to want to pull the switch!

THREE. Shut up!

EIGHT. You're a sadist. . . .

THREE [*louder*]. Shut up!

EIGHT [*her voice strong*]. You want to see this boy die because it would satisfy you personally—not because of the
facts. You disgust me.

THREE [*shouting*]. Will you shut up! [*Lunges at* EIGHT, *but
is caught by two of the* JURORS *and is held. She struggles*

as EIGHT *watches calmly. Then she screams.*] Let me go!
I'll kill her! I'll kill her!

EIGHT [*softly*]. You don't really mean you'll kill me, do you?
[THREE *stops struggling now and stares at* EIGHT, *and all
the* JURORS *watch in silence, as:*]

CURTAIN

ACT THREE

AT RISE OF CURTAIN: *We see the same scene as at the end of Act Two. There has been no time lapse.* THREE *glares angrily at* EIGHT. *She is still held by two* JURORS. *After a long pause,* THREE *shakes herself loose and turns away. She walks to the window. The other* JURORS *stand around the room now; they are shocked by this display of anger. There is silence. Then the door* L *opens and the* GUARD *enters. She looks around the room.*]

GUARD. Is there anything wrong, ladies? I heard some noise.

FOREMAN. No. There's nothing wrong. [*Points to large diagram of apartment.*] You can take that back. We're finished with it. [GUARD *nods and takes diagram. She looks curiously at some of* JURORS *and then goes out.* JURORS *still are silent; some of them begin to sit down slowly at table.* FOUR *is still seated* D R. THREE *still stands at the window. She turns around now.* JURORS *look at her.*]

THREE [*loudly*]. Well, what are you looking at? [*They turn away. She goes back to her seat now.* EIGHT *puts her chair back at right end of table. Silently, rest of* JURORS, *including* FOUR *but excluding* ELEVEN, *take their seats.* TWELVE *begins to doodle on piece of paper.* TEN *blows her nose, but no one speaks. Then, finally.*]

FOUR. I don't see why we have to behave like children.

ELEVEN. Nor do I. We have a responsibility. This is a remarkable thing about democracy. That we are—what is the word?—ah, notified! That we are notified by mail to come down to this place—and decide on the guilt or innocence of a person; of a man or woman we have not known before. We have nothing to gain or lose by our verdict. This is one

of the reasons why we are strong. We should not make it a
personal thing. . . .

NINE [*slowly*]. Thank you, very much.

ELEVEN [*slightly surprised*]. Why do you thank me?

NINE. We forget. It's good to be reminded. [ELEVEN *nods
and leans against wall again.*]

FOUR. I'm glad that we're going to be civilized about this.

TWELVE. Well, we're still nowhere.

EIGHT. No, we're somewhere, or getting there—maybe.

FOUR. Maybe.

TWELVE. Who's got an idea?

SIX. I think maybe we should try another vote. [*Turns to
FOREMAN.*] Madam Foreman?

FOREMAN. It's all right with me. Anybody doesn't want to
vote? [*Looks around table. Most of them shake their heads.
ELEVEN has moved to table and taken her seat.*]

FOUR. Let's vote.

TWELVE. Yes, vote.

SEVEN. So all right, let's do it.

THREE. I want an open ballot. Let's call out our votes. I want
to know who stands where.

FOREMAN. That sounds fair. Anyone object? [*Looks around.
There is a general shaking of heads.*] All right. I'll call off
your jury numbers. [*Takes a pencil and paper and makes
marks in one of two columns after each vote.*] I vote guilty.
Number two?

TWO. Not guilty.

FOREMAN. Three?

THREE. Guilty.

FOREMAN. Four?

FOUR. Guilty.

FOREMAN. Five?

FIVE. Not guilty.

FOREMAN. Six?

SIX. Not guilty.

FOREMAN. Seven?

SEVEN. Guilty.

FOREMAN. Eight?

EIGHT. Not guilty.

FOREMAN. Nine?

NINE. Not guilty.

FOREMAN. Ten?

TEN. Guilty.

FOREMAN. Eleven?

ELEVEN. Not guilty.

FOREMAN. Twelve?

TWELVE. Guilty.

FOUR. That's six to six.

TEN [*very angrily*]. I'll tell you something. The crime is being committed right in this room.

FOREMAN. The vote is six to six.

THREE. I'm ready to walk into court right now and declare a hung jury. There's no point in this going on any more.

FOUR [*to* ELEVEN]. I'd like to know why you changed your mind. [*To* TWO.] And why you changed your mind. [*To* SIX.] And why you did. There are six women here who think that we may be turning a murderer loose in the streets. Emotion won't do. Why? [TWO, ELEVEN *and* SIX *look at each other.*]

SIX. It would seem that the old man did not see the boy run downstairs. I do not think it likely that the old man heard someone scream, "I'm going to kill you." Old men dream. And if the boy did scream that he was going to kill, then we have the authority of this person—[*Motions at* THREE.] —to prove that it might not really mean he's going to kill.

SEVEN. Why don't we take it in to the judge and let the boy take his chances with twelve other jurors?

FOREMAN. Six to six. I don't think we'll ever agree—on anything.

THREE. It's got to be unanimous—[*Motions at* EIGHT.]—and we're never going to convince her.

EIGHT. At first I was alone. Now five others agree; there is a doubt.

THREE. You can't ever convince me that there's a doubt, because I know there isn't no doubt.

TWELVE. I tell you what, maybe we are a hung jury. It happens sometimes.

EIGHT. We are not going to be a hung jury.

SEVEN. But we are, right now, a perfect balance. Let's take it in to the judge.

FOUR [to EIGHT]. If there is a reasonable doubt, I don't see it.

NINE. The doubt is there, in my mind.

FOREMAN. Maybe we should vote.

TWELVE. What do you mean—vote?

THREE. Not again!

TEN. I still want to know—vote on what?

FOREMAN. Are we, or aren't we, a hung jury?

EIGHT. You mean that we vote yes, we are a hung jury, or no, we are not a hung jury?

FOREMAN. That's just what I was thinking of.

FOUR. I'm not sure that we could agree on whether or not we're a hung jury.

ELEVEN. We can't even agree about whether or not the window should be open.

FOREMAN. Let's make it a majority vote. The majority wins.

FOUR. If seven or more of us vote yes, that we are a hung jury, then we take it in to the judge and tell him that we are a hung jury.

FOREMAN. Right. And if seven or more vote no, that means that we aren't a hung jury, and we go on discussing it.

FOUR. It doesn't seem quite right to me.

THREE. It's the only solution.

SEVEN. I agree, it's the only way.

TWELVE. Anything to end this.

FOREMAN [looking around table]. Are we agreed then? Seven or more votes yes, and we take it in to the judge. [ALL nod.]

THREE. Let's call our votes out.

FOREMAN. I vote yes, we're a hung jury. [Makes a mark on a sheet of paper.] Two?

TWO. No.

FOREMAN. Three?

THREE. Yes.

FOREMAN. Four?

FOUR. Yes.

FOREMAN. Five?

FIVE. No.

FOREMAN. Six?

SIX. No.

FOREMAN. Seven?

SEVEN. Yes.

FOREMAN. Eight?

EIGHT. No.

FOREMAN. Nine?

NINE. No.

FOREMAN. Ten?

TEN. Yes.

FOREMAN. Eleven?

ELEVEN. No.

FOREMAN. Twelve?

TWELVE. Yes.

THREE [*screeching*]. Oh, no!

FOREMAN. It's six to six.

NINE. We can't even get a majority to decide whether or not we're a hung jury.

FOUR [*rising*]. I went along with the majority vote on this question. And I didn't agree with voting that way, not really, and I still don't. So I'm changing my vote. I say no, we are not a hung jury. I believe that the boy is guilty beyond a reasonable doubt. But there are some things I want to find out from those who changed their minds.

FOREMAN. Then we aren't a hung jury—so we go on.

EIGHT. Good! We go on.

FOUR [*to* TWO]. Why did you change your mind?

TWO [*hesitating for a moment*]. She—[*Points to* EIGHT.]— she seems so sure. And she has made a number of good points, while she—[*Points to* THREE.]—only gets mad and insults everybody.

FOUR. Does the anger and the insult change the guilt of the boy? He did do it. Are you going to turn a murderer loose because one of the jurors becomes angry when she thinks a murderer is being turned loose?

TWO. That's true.

FIVE. There is a doubt.

FOUR. I don't think so. The track is straight in front of the window. Let's take that point. So the el train would have made a low, rumbling noise. El trains screech when they go around curves. So the old man could have heard a scream, which is high-pitched. And it is a tenement and they have thin walls.

THREE. Good. Good. That's it. That's it.

FOUR. And what if the old man was wrong about the time it took him to get to the door but right about whom he saw? Please remember that there weren't any fingerprints on the knife, and it is summer, so gloves seem unlikely.

THREE [to EIGHT]. Now, I want you to listen to this lady. [Motions at FOUR.] She's talking sense.

FOUR. And it might have taken a few seconds to get a hand-kerchief out and wipe the fingerprints away.

EIGHT. This is a point.

THREE. Why don't we just time this one, to see?

FIVE. Just what are we timing?

EIGHT. Yes, let's be exact, please.

FOUR. I am saying that the old man downstairs might have been wrong about how long it took him to get to the door but that he was right about whom he saw running down the stairs. Now it may have taken the murderer about thirty-five seconds to wipe away all the fingerprints and get down the stairs to the place where the old man saw him—the boy, that is.

THREE. This is right.

FOREMAN. We reconstructed the old man getting out of bed and going to the door, and we timed that; now let's recon-struct the actual crime.

NINE. As well as we can reconstruct it.

SEVEN. I think a murderer could use up thirty or forty seconds pretty easily at that point.

FOUR. Let's reconstruct the killing.

SEVEN. Yes, let's.

THREE [*taking knife from table, giving it to* EIGHT]. Here, you do the stabbing.

FOUR [*taking knife*]. No, I'll do it.

THREE [*to* SEVEN]. Why don't you be the one that gets stabbed? And don't forget—you take one second to fall.

FOUR [*rising, moving toward* R *and turning to* SEVEN]. And he was found on his side—his right side—so fall and roll onto your right side. [*To* EIGHT.] If someone hates another person enough to kill him, don't you think that it's reasonable to suppose that the murderer would look at his victim for a second or two?

TWELVE [*to* EIGHT]. Try to divorce yourself from this particular case—just human nature.

EIGHT. Yes, it seems reasonable.

THREE. Hey, wait a minute! [ALL *look at* THREE.] He falls and he ends up on his right side, the father did; but stabbing someone isn't like shooting them, even when it's right in the heart. The father would have worked around for a few seconds—lying there on the floor—writhing, maybe.

FOUR. That's quite possible. There would have been enough oxygen in his system to carry him for two or three seconds, I should think.

ELEVEN. Wouldn't the father have cried out?

THREE. Maybe the boy held his mouth.

EIGHT. That also seems possible.

FOUR. Also, there's another point we might bring out. Anyone who is clear enough mentally to wipe the fingerprints away after murdering someone, well, that person is also clear enough mentally to look around the apartment, or the room in this case, to see if there are any other clues. It would just be for a second or two, I should think, but still he would look around.

THREE. This gets better and better.

FOUR. We're trying to make it clear. One doesn't talk about quality when murder is involved. Well, let's do it. [*Takes handkerchief from purse and puts it in sleeve of dress.*]

FOREMAN. About this on the fingerprints—the boy wiped the fingerprints off the knife. Well, what about the doorknob? If I saw a man coming into my home, a man that hated me, and if he was wiping the doorknob with a handkerchief as he came in, I'd start screaming. [ALL *smile.*] I think even a man would have an uneasy feeling. So the doorknobs must have been wiped after the killing, and this, too, would take some time.

FOUR [*to* TWO]. You timed the last one. Why don't you time this one, too?

TWO. All right.

FOUR [*as* SEVEN *takes her position in front of* FOUR *at* R *stage.* SEVEN *seems to look forward to her opportunity for dramatics.* FOUR *has knife in her hand*]. Stamp your foot when you want me to start.

TWO [*waiting a few seconds*]. I want the hand to be at sixty. [*Waits another second, then stamps her foot.*]

FOUR [*not screaming, but still loudly*]. I'm going to kill you. [*Brings knife down, overhand. Blade is collapsed.* SEVEN *catches knife in her hands and falls to floor a second after shout. She writhes a bit, then rolls onto her right side.* FOUR *stares at her for a few moments, then pulls handkerchief from her sleeve. It takes her a moment or two to shake out the handkerchief; then she bends down and wipes handle of knife. She looks about, as though checking to be sure that she has done everything. Then she rushes to door* L *that leads out of jury room and wipes doorknob. Then she turns around a full circle and wipes knob again.*] He would have wiped both knobs. [*Then she rushes* R *and then goes back to door of jury room and repeats double process on doorknob. Then she stamps her foot and cries out.*] Stop!

TWO [*checking watch*]. Twenty—yeah, twenty, twenty-five—twenty-nine—about twenty-nine and a half seconds, I'd say.

FOUR [*moving to behind* FOREMAN'S *chair at left end of*

table]. And whoever did murder the old man—and I think it was the boy—still had to run down the hall and down the stairs, at least one flight of stairs.

THREE. You see! You see! [SEVEN *rises from floor, dusts herself off and pats her hair in place.*]

FOUR. The old man downstairs may have been wrong on the time, but in view of this, I think it's quite reasonable to assume that he did see the boy run downstairs.

TWELVE [*to* EIGHT]. So now both time sequences check, the one you did and the one we did; what with running downstairs and everything, it does pretty much check out on times.

SEVEN. Sure, he's an old man who wants attention. . . . [*Motions at* NINE.] She's probably right, but the old man feels the way everyone does—a life is at stake.

FOUR. So the story of the old man may well be true.

EIGHT. Except for the fact that he absolutely swore, under oath, that it was only fifteen seconds.

NINE. We seem to all agree that it was twenty-five to thirty-five seconds later.

EIGHT. You are now admitting that the old man lied in one case and told the truth in the other. I admit that this does tend to confirm the story of the old man, but in part he is now a proven liar—and this is by your own admission.

TWO [*to* EIGHT]. That may be true, that the old man lies in part, but I think it will change my vote once more. [*To* FOREMAN.] Guilty.

THREE [*to* SIX]. What about you? What do you think now?

SIX [*getting up, crossing to water cooler*]. I'm not just sure what I think. I want to talk some more. At first I thought guilty, then I changed. Now—I'm sort of swinging back to guilty. [*Takes a drink.*]

THREE [*to* ELEVEN]. And what about you?

ELEVEN. No. [*Shakes her head.*] I am now in real doubt— real doubt. . . .

FIVE. I say guilty. I was right the first time.

THREE. Now we're beginning to make sense in here.

FOREMAN. It seems to be about nine guilty to three not guilty. [*FOUR sits again.*]

EIGHT. One more question about the old man downstairs. How many of you live in apartment buildings? [*Eight hands go up, including her own.*]

ELEVEN [*to* EIGHT]. I don't know what you're thinking, but I know what I'm thinking.

FOUR [*to* ELEVEN]. What's that?

ELEVEN. I do not live in a tenement, but it is close, and there is just enough light in the hall so you can see the steps, no more—the light bulbs are so small—and this murder took place in a tenement. Remember how we stumbled on the steps?

EIGHT. The police officers were using big bulbs, and one even had a flashlight. Remember?

ELEVEN. An old man who misjudged the time by twenty seconds, on this we all agree, this old man looked down the dark hallway of a tenement and recognized a running figure.

EIGHT. He was one hundred per cent wrong about the time; it took twice as long as he thought.

ELEVEN. Then could not the old man be one hundred per cent wrong about who he saw?

THREE. That's the most stupid thing I've ever heard of. You're making that up out of thin air.

TWELVE. We're a hung jury. Let's be honest about it.

ELEVEN [*to* SEVEN]. Do you truly feel that there is no room for reasonable doubt?

SEVEN. Yes, I do.

ELEVEN. I beg your pardon, but maybe you don't understand the term, "reasonable doubt."

SEVEN [*angrily*]. What do you mean, I don't understand it? Who do you think you are to talk to me like that? [*To* ALL.] How do you like this babe? She comes over here running for her life, and before she can even take a big breath she's telling us how to run our lives. The nerve of her!

FOUR. No one here is asking where anyone came from.

SEVEN. I was born right here.

FOUR. Or where your mother came from. [*Looks at* SEVEN, *who looks away.*]

EIGHT. Maybe it wouldn't hurt us to take a few tips from people who come running here! Maybe they learned something we don't know. We're not so perfect.

ELEVEN. Please. . . . I am used to this. . . . It's all right. Thank you.

EIGHT. It's not all right.

SEVEN. Okay—okay—I apologize. Is that what you want?

EIGHT [*grimly*]. That's what I want.

FOREMAN. All right. Let's stop the arguing. Who's got something constructive to say?

TWO [*hesitantly*]. Well, something's been bothering me a little. This whole business about the stab wound, and how it was made—the downward angle of it, you know?

THREE. Don't tell me we're gonna start on that. They went over it and over it in court.

TWO. I know they did—but I don't go along with it. The boy is five feet eight inches tall. His father was six feet two inches tall. That's a difference of six inches. It's a very awkward thing to stab *down* into the chest of someone who's half a foot taller than you are. [THREE *grabs knife from table and jumps up.*]

THREE [*moving* L C]. Look, you're not going to be satisfied till you see it again. I'm going to give you a demonstration. Somebody get up. [*Looks toward table.* EIGHT *stands up and walks toward her.* THREE *closes knife, puts it in pocket of her dress. They stand face to face and look at each other for a moment.*] Okay. [*To* TWO.] Now watch this. I don't want to have to do it again. [*Crouches down until she is quite a bit shorter than* EIGHT.] Is that six inches?

TWELVE. That's more than six inches.

THREE. Okay, let it be more. [*Reaches into her pocket and takes out knife. She flips it open, changes its position in her hand and holds knife aloft, ready to stab. She and* EIGHT *look steadily into each other's eyes. Then* THREE *stabs downward, hard.*]

TWO [*shouting*]. Look out! [*Reaches short just as the blade reaches* EIGHT'S *chest. Two or three of the jurors let out small screams and gasps.* THREE *laughs.*]

SIX. That's not funny. [*Crosses back to table and sits.*]

FIVE. What's the matter with you?

THREE. Now, just calm down. Nobody's hurt, are they?

EIGHT [*low*]. No. Nobody's hurt. [*Turns, crosses back to her place, but does not sit.*]

THREE. All right. There's your angle. Take a look at it. [*Illustrates.*] Down and in. That's how I'd stab a taller person in the chest, and that's how it was done. [*Crosses back to her place at table.*] Take a look at it, and tell me I'm wrong. [TWO *doesn't answer.* THREE *looks at her a moment, then jams knife into table and sits down.* ALL *look at knife.*]

SIX. Down and in. I guess there's no argument. [EIGHT *picks knife out of table and closes it. She flicks it open and, changing its position in her hand, stabs downward with it.*]

EIGHT [*to* SIX]. Did you ever stab anyone?

SIX. Of course not.

EIGHT [*to* THREE]. Did you?

THREE. All right, let's not be silly.

EIGHT [*insistently*]. Did you?

THREE [*loudly*]. No. I didn't!

EIGHT. Where do you get all your information about how it's done?

THREE. What do you mean? It's just common sense.

EIGHT. Have you ever seen a person stabbed?

THREE [*pausing, looking around the room rather nervously; then, finally*]. No.

EIGHT. All right. I want to ask you something. The boy was an experienced knife-fighter. He was even sent to reform school for knifing someone. Isn't that so?

TWELVE. That's right.

EIGHT. Look at this. [*Closes knife, flicks it open, and changes position of knife so that she can stab overhand.*] Doesn't it seem like an awkward way to handle a knife?

THREE. What are you asking me for? [EIGHT *closes blade and flicks it open, holding the knife ready to slash under-handed.*]

FIVE. Wait a minute! What's the matter with me? Give me that knife. [*Reaches out for knife.*]

EIGHT. Have you ever seen a knife fight?

FIVE. Yes, I have.

EIGHT. In the movies? [*Passes knife to* FIVE.]

FIVE. In my backyard. On my stoop. In the vacant lot across the street. Too many of them. Switch knives came with the neighborhood where I lived. Funny that I didn't think of it before. I guess you try to forget those things. [*Flicks knife open.*] Anyone who's ever used a switch knife would never have stabbed downward. You don't handle a switch knife that way. You use it underhanded. [*Illustrates.*]

EIGHT. Then he couldn't have made the kind of wound that killed his father.

FIVE. I suppose it's conceivable that he could have made the wound, but it's not likely, not if he'd ever had any experience with switch knives; and we know that the boy had a lot of experience with switch knives.

THREE. I don't believe it.

TEN. Neither do I. You're giving us a lot of mumbo-jumbo.

EIGHT [*to* TWELVE]. What do you think?

TWELVE [*hesitantly*]. Well—I don't know.

EIGHT [*to* SEVEN]. What about you?

SEVEN. Listen, I'll tell you all something. I'm a little sick of this whole thing already. We're getting nowhere fast. Let's stop all this arguing and go home.

EIGHT. Before we decide anything more, I would like to try to pull this together.

THREE. This should be good.

FOUR. She has a right. Let her go ahead.

TWO. Do you want me to time this, too? [EIGHT *looks at* TWO.]

FOREMAN. Let's hear her.

TWELVE [*getting comfortable*]. I'm in advertising. I love to see things pulled together. Makes for good layouts. Let's

try to look at the whole picture to see if some pattern is
there. Maybe we could try getting a fresh point of view.

EIGHT. I want you all to look at this logically and consistently.

THREE. We have. Guilty.

EIGHT. I want to know—is the boy smart or is the boy dumb?

FOUR. What do you mean?

EIGHT [*moving* U C, *so that she is standing back of women at
upstage side of table*]. This is a boy who has gone to reform
school for knife fighting. The night of the murder he bought
a knife, a switch knife. It would then take a very stupid boy
to go and murder a man, his father, with an instrument that
everyone would associate with the son.

THREE. I quite agree, he's dumb.

EIGHT. However, if he were dumb, then why did he make the
kind of wound that an inexperienced man would make with
a knife?

FOREMAN. I'm not sure I understand.

EIGHT. To murder someone must take a great emotion, great
hatred. [*Moves over to left of* FOREMAN.] And at that moment he would handle the knife as best he could, and a
trained knife-fighter would handle it as he had been trained,
underhand. . . . [*Makes underhanded motion.*] A man
who had not been trained would go overhand. . . . [*Makes
overhanded motion.*] But the boy is being very smart. Everyone knows that he is an experienced knife-fighter—so he is
smart enough at that moment to make the wound that an
amateur would make. That boy is a smart one. Smart enough
to wipe the fingerprints away, perhaps even smart enough to
wait until an el train was going by in order to cover the
noise. Now, is the boy smart, or is he dumb? [*Looks
around.*]

THREE. Hey, now, wait a minute!

NINE. Well, the woman across the el tracks saw the murder
through the el train, so someone in that el train could have
seen the murder, too.

EIGHT. A possibility, but no one did that we know of.

NINE. It would take an awfully dumb man to take that chance, doing the murder as the train went by.

EIGHT. Exactly. A dumb man, a very stupid man, a man swept by emotion. Probably he heard nothing; he probably didn't even hear the train coming. And whoever did murder the father did it as well as he could.

FOUR. So?

EIGHT [*moving back to her place, at right end of table, not sitting*]. The boy is dumb enough to do everything to associate himself with the switch knife—a switch knife murder —and then a moment after the murder he becomes smart. The boy is smart enough to make a kind of wound that would lead us to suspect someone else, and yet at the same instant he is dumb enough to do the killing as an el train is going by—and then a moment later, he is smart enough to wipe fingerprints away. To make this boy guilty you have to say he is dumb from eight o'clock until about midnight, and then about midnight he is smart one second, then dumb for a few seconds and then smart again and then once again he becomes stupid, so stupid that he does not think of a good alibi. Now, is this boy smart or is he dumb? To say that he is guilty you have to toss his intelligence like a pancake. There is doubt, doubt, doubt. [*Beats table with fist as she emphasizes word "doubt."*]

FOUR. I hadn't thought of that.

EIGHT. And the old man downstairs. On the stand he swore that it was fifteen seconds. He insisted on fifteen seconds, but we all agree that it must have been almost forty seconds.

NINE. Does the old man lie half of the time and then does he tell the truth the other half of the time?

EIGHT. For the boy to be guilty he must be stupid, then smart, then stupid and then smart and so on; and also, for the boy to be guilty the old man downstairs must be a liar half of the time and the other half of the time he must tell the truth. You can reasonably doubt. [*Sits again. There is a moment of silence.*]

SEVEN [*breaking silence*]. I'm sold on "reasonable doubt."

TWO. I think I am, too.

SIX. I wanted more talk, and now I've had it.

EIGHT [*fast*]. I want another vote.

FOREMAN. Okay, there's another vote called for. I guess the quickest way is a show of hands. Anybody object? [*No one does.*] All right. All those voting not guilty raise your hands. *Jurors* TWO, FIVE, SIX, SEVEN, EIGHT, NINE, ELEVEN *and* TWELVE *raise their hands immediately.* FOREMAN *looks around table carefully, then she too raises her hand. She looks around table, counting silently.*] Nine. [*Hands go down.*] All those voting guilty. [*Jurors* THREE, FOUR *and* TEN *raise their hands.*] Three. [*They lower their hands.*] The vote is nine to three in favor of acquittal.

TEN. I don't understand you people. How can you believe this boy is innocent? Look, you know how those people lie. I don't have to tell you. They don't know what the truth is. And let me tell you, they—[FIVE *gets up from table, turns her back to it and goes to window.*]—don't need any real big reason to kill someone, either. You know, they get drunk, and bang, someone's lying in the gutter. Nobody's blaming them. That's how they are. You know what I mean? Violent! [NINE *gets up, goes to window and looks out. She is followed by* ELEVEN.] Human life don't mean as much to them as it does to us. Hey, where are you all going? Look, these people're drinking and fighting all the time, and if somebody gets killed, so somebody gets killed. They don't care. Oh, sure, there are some good things about them, too. Look, I'm the first to say that. [EIGHT *gets up, then* TWO *and* SIX *follow her to window.*] I've known a few who were pretty decent, but that's the exception. Most of them, it's like they have no feelings. They can do anything. What's going on here? [FOREMAN *gets up and goes to window, followed by* SEVEN *and* TWELVE.] I'm speaking my piece, and you—listen to me! They're no good. There's not a one of 'em who's any good. We better watch out. Take it from me. This boy on trial—[THREE *sits at table toying with knife as* FOUR *gets up and starts toward* TEN. *All other*

JURORS *have their backs turned on* TEN.] Well, don't you know about them? Listen to me! What are you doing? I'm trying to tell you something. . . . [FOUR *stands over her as she trails off. There is a dead silence. Then* FOUR *speaks softly.*]

FOUR. I've had enough. If you open your mouth again, I'm going to scratch your eyes out. [FOUR *stands there and looks at* TEN. *No one moves or speaks.* TEN *looks at* FOUR *and then looks down at table.*]

TEN [*softly*]. I'm only trying to tell you. . . . [*There is a long pause as* FOUR *stares down at* TEN.]

FOUR [*to* JURORS *at window*]. All right. Sit down, everybody. [ALL *move back to their seats. When they are seated,* FOUR *takes a stand behind women on upstage side of table. She speaks quietly.*] I still believe the boy is guilty of murder. I'll tell you why. To me, the most damning evidence was given by the woman across the street who claimed that she actually saw the murder committed.

THREE. That's right. As far as I'm concerned, that's the most important testimony.

EIGHT. All right. Let's go over her testimony. What exactly did she say?

FOUR [*moving toward window*]. I believe I can recount it accurately. She said that she went to bed at about eleven o'clock that night. Her bed was next to the open window and she could look out of the window while lying down and see directly into the window across the street. She tossed and turned for over an hour, unable to fall asleep. Finally she turned toward the window at about 12:10 and, as she looked out, she saw the boy stab his father. As far as I can seen, this is unshakable testimony.

THREE. That's what I mean. That's the whole case. [FOUR *takes off her eyeglasses and begins to polish them as they all sit silently watching her.*]

FOUR [*to* ALL]. Frankly, in view of this, I don't see how you can vote for acquittal. [*To* TWELVE, *as she sits again.*] What do you think about it?

TWELVE. Well—maybe . . . there's so much evidence to sift. . . .

THREE. What do you mean, maybe? She's absolutely right. You can throw out all the other evidence.

FOUR. That was my feeling. I don't deny the validity of the points that she's made. [*Motions at* EIGHT.] Shall we say that on one side of the tracks there is doubt? But what can you say about the story of the woman? She saw it. [TWO, *while polishing her glasses, too, squints at the clock.*]

TWO. What time is it?

ELEVEN. Ten minutes of six.

SIX. You don't suppose they'd let us go home and finish it in the morning? My little girl has the mumps. . . .

FIVE. Not a chance.

EIGHT [*to* TWO]. Can't you see the clock without your glasses?

TWO. Not clearly.

EIGHT. Oh.

FOUR. Glasses are a nuisance, aren't they?

EIGHT [*an edge of excitement in her tone*]. Well, what do you all do when you wake up at night and want to know what time it is?

TWO. I put on my glasses and look at the clock.

FOUR. I just lie in bed and wait for the clock to chime. My father gave it to me when we were married, my husband and I. It was ten years before we had a place to put it.

EIGHT [*to* TWO]. Do you wear your glasses to bed?

TWO. Of course not. No one wears glasses to bed.

EIGHT. The woman who testified that she saw the killing wears glasses. What about her?

FOUR. Did she wear glasses?

ELEVEN [*excitedly*]. Of course! The woman wore bifocals. I remember this very clearly. They looked quite strong.

NINE. That's right. Bifocals. She never took them off.

FOUR. Funny. I never thought of that.

EIGHT. I think it's logical to say that she was not wearing her glasses in bed, and I don't think she'd put them on to glance casually out of the window. She testified that the murder took place the instant she looked out, and that the lights went out a split second later. She couldn't have had time to put on her glasses then. Now, perhaps this woman honestly thought she saw the boy kill his father. [*Rises.*] I say that she only saw a blur.

THREE. How do you know what she saw? Maybe she's far-sighted. . . . [*Looks around. No one answers. Loudly.*] How does she—[*Motions at* EIGHT.]—know all these things? [*There is silence.*]

EIGHT. Does anyone think there still is not a reasonable doubt? [*Looks around room, then squarely at* TEN. TEN *looks down at table for a moment, then looks up at* EIGHT.]

TEN. I will always wonder. But there is a reasonable doubt.

THREE [*loudly*]. I think he's guilty!

EIGHT [*calmly*]. Does anyone else?

FOUR [*quietly*]. No. I'm convinced now. There is a reasonable doubt.

EIGHT [*to* THREE]. You're alone.

FOREMAN. Eleven votes, not guilty; one, guilty.

THREE. I don't care whether I'm alone or not! I have a right. . . .

EIGHT. Yes, you have a right. [ALL *stare at* THREE.]

THREE. Well, I told you. I think the boy's guilty. What else do you want?

EIGHT. Your arguments. [ALL *look at* THREE *after glancing at* EIGHT.]

THREE. I gave you my arguments.

EIGHT. We're not convinced. We're waiting to hear them again. We have time. [*Sits down again.* THREE *runs to* FOUR, *grabs her arm.*]

THREE [*pleading*]. Listen. What's the matter with you? You're the one who made all the arguments. You can't turn now. A guilty man's going to be walking the streets. A murderer. He's got to die! Stay with me! . . .

FOUR [*rising*]. I'm sorry. I'm convinced. I don't think I'm wrong very often, but I guess I was this once. [*Crosses* R.] There is a reasonable doubt in my mind.

EIGHT. We're waiting. . . . [THREE *turns violently on her.*]

THREE [*shouting*]. You're not going to sway me! [ALL *are*

staring at THREE.] I'm entitled to my opinion! [*No one answers her.*] It's going to be a hung jury! [*Turns abruptly, sits in her chair again.*] That's it!

EIGHT. There's nothing we can do about that except hope that some night, maybe in a few months, why, you might be able to get some sleep.

FIVE. You're all alone.

NINE. It takes a great deal of courage to stand alone.

FOUR [*moving back to table, sitting*]. If it is a hung jury, there will be another trial, and some of us will point these things out to the various lawyers. [THREE *looks around table at all of them. As* THREE'S *glance goes from juror to juror, each one of them shakes her head in* THREE'S *direction. Then, suddenly,* THREE'S *face contorts and she begins to pound on the table with her fist. She is half crying.*]

THREE [*shrieking*]. All right! [*Jumps up quickly and moves* ⋂ R, *her back to all of them, as* FOREMAN *goes to door* L *and knocks. The other* JURORS *now rise.*]

[*The* GUARD *opens the door and looks in and sees them all standing. The* GUARD *holds the door open for them as they all file past and out* L; *that is, all except* THREE *and* EIGHT. *The* GUARD *waits for them.* EIGHT *moves toward door* L, *pausing at* L C.]

EIGHT [*to* THREE]. They're waiting. [THREE *sees that she is alone. She moves to table and pulls switch knife out of table and walks over to* EIGHT *with it.* THREE *is holding knife in approved knife-fighter fashion.* THREE *looks long and hard at* EIGHT, *and weaves a bit from side to side as she holds knife with point of it in the direction of* EIGHT'S *stomach.* EIGHT *speaks quietly, but firmly.*] Not guilty. [THREE *turns knife around and* EIGHT *takes it by handle. She closes knife and puts it in her purse.*]

THREE. Not guilty! [THREE *walks out of room.* EIGHT *glances around quickly, sighs, then turns and moves out through door.* GUARD *goes out, closing door.*]

CURTAIN